SEARCH AND DISCOVER
BY
Q.L. PEARCE
SCIENCE FUN BOOKS

PREHISTORIC MAMMALS

Illustrated by Jerry Tiritilli

TOR

A TOM DOHERTY ASSOCIATES BOOK
NEW YORK

**Don't miss the other
Search and Discover Science Fun Books**

**MY BODY AND HOW IT WORKS
OUR SOLAR SYSTEM AND BEYOND
SNAKES AND OTHER REPTILES**

A TOR Book
Published by Tom Doherty Associates, Inc.
49 West 24 Street
New York, NY 10010

ISBN: 0-812-59493-2   Can. ISBN: 0-812-59494-0

First edition: February 1989

Printed in the United States of America

0 9 8 7 6 5 4 3 2 1

The animals that you see today did not always appear this way. Prehistoric mammals—the ancestors to most mammals that live today—gradually changed, or evolved, into such modern animals as dogs, horses, elephants, whales, and bats. This evolution took millions of years. In this book you will learn many fascinating facts about prehistoric mammals.

What Is a Mammal?

A Warm-Blooded Animal That Has Hair and Feeds Its Young with Milk from Its Body

There are three kinds of mammals today. The most primitive group of mammals are the *monotremes*, which are the egg-laying mammals. They do not give birth to live young but actually hatch their young from eggs. The duck-billed platypus and the spiny anteater or echidna are monotremes. The second group of living mammals are the *marsupials*, or pouched mammals, such as the kangaroo and the koala. The young of these mammals are born alive but are very tiny and immature. They crawl up their mother's body and into her pouch, where they live until they have developed. Most monotremes and marsupials live in or near Australia. The last group of mammals is the largest and most familiar to us. They are the *placentals*. The young of these animals are born alive but are much more developed at birth than are the marsupials. Most of the mammals that we know today, including dogs, cats, horses, cows, monkeys, and human beings, are placentals.

What Is a Prehistoric Mammal?
A Mammal That Lived Before Recorded History

Mammals began to evolve at the end of the first part of the Mesozoic era. This period was known as the Age of Reptiles because dinosaurs and other reptiles were numerous. But it was not until after the dinosaurs became extinct that mammals became as plentiful as the reptiles had been.

How Do We Know About Prehistoric Mammals?

From Fossils

A fossil is any trace of a living thing that has been preserved. Usually fossils are preserved in rocks, but some Ice Age mammals have been preserved in ice and even in tar! A fossil can be a footprint, skin impression, bones, or shells. Some fossils have been replaced by minerals, turning them to "stones." Most mammal fossils consist of bones and teeth. Scientists who study fossils are called *paleontologists*. They compare fossil bones with the bones of present-day animals. Paleontologists work with artists to reconstruct the skeleton, the muscles, and body coverings of prehistoric mammals.

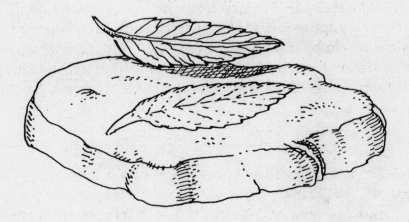

How Do We Know How Old Fossils Are?

From Scientists Who Use Radioactivity to Date Fossils

Fossils are deposited in layers called strata. These layers are put down in order, with the oldest on the bottom and the newest on the top. Scientists know that radioactive minerals decay or break down at different rates. Thus, they test the radioactive minerals in these strata to determine their age and the age of the fossils that they contain.

DISCOVERY CORNER: You can make your own plant fossil. You will need a leaf and some soft clay. First, flatten a piece of soft clay so that it is bigger than your leaf. Press the leaf into the clay. Carefully lift the leaf from the clay. Let the clay harden. The impression left by the leaf in the clay is similar to the mold made by a prehistoric leaf that was covered by sediment and then turned to rock over time. Did you leave any fingerprints in the clay? If you did, you would have a mammal fossil, too!

FUN FACT: In 1977 in Siberia, a part of Russia, a baby mammoth was found frozen in a glacier. All of its body— bones, muscles, skin, hair, even the last meal in its stomach— was preserved!

How Did Mammals Evolve?
From Mammal-Like Reptiles

Although it is difficult to say exactly which mammal was the first, scientists know that some reptiles developed mammal-like characteristics. Dimetrodon was probably one of the first mammal-like reptiles. It had a tall, spiny fin that projected from its backbone. Scientists think that dimetrodon used that fin to help regulate its body temperature. Living reptiles are cold-blooded, which means that their body temperature varies with the environment. To be active, they must raise their body temperatures by warming themselves in the sun. If they get too hot, they must look for shade. Dimetrodon's temperature regulation was a little better. Its fin probably had a lot of blood vessels in it, so when it wanted to warm up it faced the fin to the sun and increased the blood supply to the fin, thus warming its body rapidly. It was a meat eater thus giving it a head start over its prey. Dimetrodon may have been able to shut down the flow of blood in its body when the air was too warm. This would slow down the warming or retain heat longer in the evening. In this way, dimetrodon could stay active after the other reptiles had become sluggish.

Mammal-like reptiles like dimetrodon gave rise to the therapsids, also mammal-like reptiles. Cynognathus was a therapsid that lived 240 to 248 million years ago. Most reptiles have teeth that are about the same size and shape, but mammals often have specialized teeth, some for chewing or grinding, some for biting or tearing. Cynognathus, although a reptile, had mammal-like teeth. Many scientists believe that reptiles like Cynognathus were the ancestors to all mammals.

When Did the First Mammals Appear on Earth?

As Early As 200 Million Years Ago

With the rise of the dinosaurs, most of the mammal-like reptiles became extinct. The only mammal-like reptiles to survive were small, rodentlike insect eaters. Most scientists think that these animals gradually evolved into true mammals. Two examples of insect-eating mammals are Deltatheridium and Amphitherium. They lived in the trees and underbrush and probably lived among the dinosaurs much the same way as insect-eating mammals live among the larger mammals today. Many scientists think that mammals like Deltatheridium gave rise to all of the other placental mammals. Similar animals alive today are shrews, moles, and hedgehogs.

FUN FACT: In the Greek language, the word *therium* means a wild beast. Many animals whose names end in *therium* are mammals.

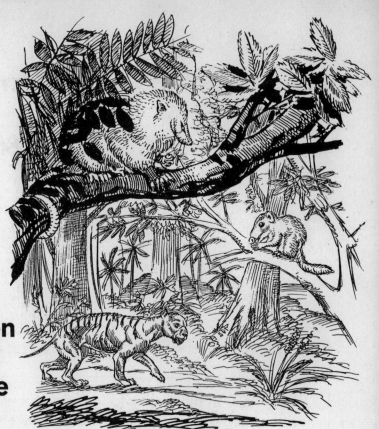

What Was the Earth Like When Mammals and Dinosaurs Were First Evolving?

The Continents Formed a Single Landmass, and the Climate Was Similar Everywhere

Throughout the Mesozoic era, the Earth's climate was warm and moist. During the Triassic period, 248 to 213 million years ago, all of the continents were connected in one large landmass called Pangea. Animals could live and roam over wide areas. During the Jurassic period, 213 to 144 million years ago, the landmass began to break up, and the southernmost parts began to separate from the northern. During the Cretaceous period, from 144 to 65 million years ago, the northern and southern continents were completely separate. Australia and Antarctica formed a separate landmass from the other continents. Mammals in those areas were separated from other mammals. Primitive marsupials have arrived very well in Australia because they were isolated from more advanced placental mammals. Except for the family of mammals that include the opossum living in North and South America, marsupials are almost nonexistent in the rest of the world.

Were All of the Early Mammals Insect Eaters?

No, Some of Them Had Begun to Eat Plants

In the late Jurassic period, the first plant-eating mammals appeared. They were rodentlike mammals called *multituberculates*. Their teeth were quite rodentlike. In this time period the *pantotheres* also appeared. This group included the ancestors to most later mammals. Their teeth could both slice and crush food, so they could eat a varied diet of insects and fruit. It was from the pantotheres that the two major lines of living mammals—the marsupials and the placentals—evolved. But it was not until about 115 million years later, during the Cenozoic era, that the mammals truly dominated the Earth.

What Is the Cenozoic Era?

The Cenozoic Era Is Also Known As the Age of Mammals

The Cenozoic era is made up of 7 time groupings, called epochs. They are the Paleocene, from 65 to 55 million years ago; the Eocene, from 55 to 38 million years ago; the Oligocene, from 38 to 25 million years ago; the Miocene, from 25 to 5 million years ago; the Pliocene, from 5 to 2 million years ago; the Pleistocene, from 2 million to about 10,000 years ago; and the Holocene, the epoch of the last 10,000 years.

FUN FACT: The Paleocene epoch was named in 1874 by Wilhelm Philipp Schimper, a German scientist.

What Was the Earth Like at the Start of the Cenozoic Era?

The Earth Was Like a Tropical Rain Forest

Sixty-five million years ago, the Earth's climate was warm and wet. The seas that had covered much of the Earth had begun to shrink, and there was more land. Tropical ferns and other leafy plants covered the Earth. Great land-masses, which became the Earth's continents, were drifting apart. Australia, Antarctica, and South America were separated from all the other continents. North America, Europe, and Asia remained joined. Most modern mammals are descended from the prehistoric mammals that lived on this giant landmass.

After the Dinosaurs Died Out, What Did Prehistoric Mammals Look Like?

Most Mammals Were Small

While the dinosaurs were still alive, many mammals were active only at night. Most of them ate insects. After the dinosaurs became extinct, mammals began to change and adapt to different ways of life. They came out in the daylight and ate a variety of different foods. Many mammals had heavy heads, short legs, and five-toed feet with thick toenails.

DISCOVERY CORNER: Sayings or expressions are often used to compare human behavior to animal behavior. Many of these expressions are about mammals. There is truth to some, but others are nothing more than "mammal myths." You will need to go to the library or use an encyclopedia to answer these questions: Which of the following expressions are based on truth? Which are mammal myths?

- "blind as a bat"
- "playing dead like an opossum"
- "quiet as a mouse"
- "dirty as a pig"

Can you think of other expressions about mammals? Are they true or false?

Did Early Mammals Change Quickly After the Dinosaurs Died?

No, a Long Time Passed Before Any Noticeable Change Took Place

Primitive hedgehogs were very successful feeding on insects and worms at night, and thus there was little pressure to change. Opossums, with their generalized diet and ability to adapt to change, were also very successful. Like today's opossum, the prehistoric opossum had a prehensile tail (a tail that can grab and hold things), and it carried its young in a pouch. But slowly, some groups of animals began to change or evolve.

What Did the First Cenozoic Mammals Eat?

Mostly Insects, but Plant Eaters and Meat Eaters Were Beginning to Evolve

There are more insects than any other group of organisms in the world, so it is not surprising that most of the Mesozoic mammals were insect eaters. The earliest known placental mammals, called Proteutheria, were insect eaters. With the extinction of the dinosaurs, many other foods and living spaces became available to the mammals. The early primates began eating plants. This was made easy by their fingers and toes with which they could grasp. Ant-eating animals appeared. Plant eaters like squirrels and early forms of rabbits appeared. Around this same time, meat eaters also began to appear. They evolved specialized teeth for shearing flesh. However, the most feared predator of this era was not a mammal, but a large, flightless bird called Diatryma, which didn't have teeth.

FUN FACT: Three million different insect species live on Earth today!

What Is the Eocene Epoch?

A Time When Mammals Became Well Established on Land, in the Air, and in the Sea

The Eocene epoch followed the Paleocene epoch and lasted from about 55 to 38 million years ago. The climate during the Eocene was moist and warm and much less varied than it is today. Most areas of the world were subtropical. South America, Africa, India, and Australia were still separate from the northern continents and from each other. Mammals in these areas evolved in isolation. North America, Europe, and eastern Asia were connected. During the Eocene an early primate called Notharctus appeared. Monkeys evolved separately in African and South America.

When Did Bats Evolve?
During the Eocene Epoch

At the end of the Paleocene, the first epoch of the Cenozoic, most mammals still lived in the trees and undergrowth, but others did not. Some of the insect-eating mammals evolved into fliers. Bats evolved. They could not compete with the many kinds of birds active during the day, but at night they were able to feed on insects and fruit. They had developed a special way of finding their way around in the dark, by making sounds and listening as the sounds bounced off objects. This is called echolocation.

DISCOVERY CORNER: Try a human version of echolocation. You'll need a friend, a blindfold, and a dark area. Put on the blindfold and turn around three times. Meanwhile, your friend moves to an undisclosed location nearby. Now you clap, call out, or snap your fingers twice. Your friend repeats, or echoes, your sound. By listening to the echo, can you find the exact location where your friend is standing? Take turns with the echo game!

What Other Mammals Evolved During the Eocene?

Rodents, Other Plant Eaters, and Meat Eaters

The true rodents, with chisel-like front teeth that continue to grow throughout their lives, appeared during the Eocene. Teeth that never wear away are ideal for eating tough plant materials. Rodents soon replaced most of the rodentlike primates. The only primates left were the less-specialized early primates that could eat a variety of foods, including fruits, birds, and eggs.

Other plant eaters became larger and more numerous during the Eocene. Phenacodus, a condylarth, was a plant eater about the size of a large dog. It was different from other condylarths because it had hooves on its toes instead of claws.

What Were the Meat Eaters of the Eocene?

Mesonychids, Oxyaenids, Hyaenodonts, Artocyonids, and Miacids

The doglike mesonychids, such as Andrewsarchus, became good runners. Many of them probably hunted in packs as dogs do today. The catlike oxyaenids, such as Patriofelis, had powerful shoulders and legs that enabled them to pounce on prey. Some of these catlike and doglike prehistoric mammals groups grew. The mongooselike hyaenodonts stayed small, and slightly built—about the size of a fox—so that they could hunt in dense undergrowth. The bearlike arctocyonids fed on plants and meat much like modern bears, although they are not related to modern bears. The miacids, small-sized hunters that lived in trees, are thought to be the common ancestors of modern dogs and cats. Their descendants became the chief meat eaters of the next epoch, the Oligocene.

DISCOVERY CORNER: Human beings are omnivores; they eat both plants and meat. However, some people choose to eat only plants. They are called vegetarians. Think of the meals you ate last week. Are you an omnivore or a vegetarian?

Besides Phenacodus, What Were Other Plant Eaters of the Eocene?

The Odd-Toed Hoofed Mammals and Even-Toed Hoofed Mammals

Pantodonts continued to live in streams and lakes. One evolved to a huge size. Its name was Coryphodon. It was over 9 feet long and lived like a hippopotamus and spent most of its life in the water. Rhinoceros-sized, giant uintatheres like Uintatherium and Eobasilus, had bony knobs on their heads and looked very strange. Odd-toed hoofed mammals include the first tapirs, horses, and rhinoceroses. One giant hoofed mammal was called Brontotherium, or "thunder beast." It was over 15 feet long and weighed as much as 4 tons. It was a member of a group of large mammals called titanotheres. It had primitive teeth and lived on soft plants. It probably became extinct when the climate changed and plants became harder to chew.

Even-toed hoofed mammals include pigs, peccaries, hippopotamuses, camels, llamas, deer, antelopes, cattle, goats, sheep, and giraffes. They have an even number of toes, two or four, on each foot, which often appear to be divided in two or cloven. Most early even-toed hoofed mammals probably looked and acted like pigs.

FUN FACT: The very first fossil of an odd-toed hoofed mammal ever found was called Hyracotherium. It was the earliest known horse.

Why Do So Many Animals Seem to Evolve into Larger and Larger Forms?

Because Large Animals Have Fewer Enemies and Are More Likely to Survive

Many animals as they evolved over time tended to increase in size. Unless there was some advantage to staying small (such as to avoid being seen and eaten by a predator), animals tended to evolve into larger and larger forms as long as there was enough food to support them. Stronger animals usually survive longer and produce more young. Sometimes they get very large, like the titanothere Brontotherium.

How Did the Modern Horse Evolve?

From Hyracotherium, the Earliest Known Horse, Which Was About the Size of a Lamb

Hyracotherium had 3 toes on each hind limb and 4 on each fore limb. Hyracotherium ran on its toes, which had small hooves on them. It lived in swampy forest areas in North America, Europe, and Asia and ate soft plants. These early horses died out in Europe and Asia, but did very well in North America and began to grow larger. Hyracotherium gave rise to Orohippus, which gave rise to Mesohippus, which was about dog-sized. Besides increasing in size, horses were also developing stronger teeth so that they could eat the tougher grasses growing on extensive grasslands. Mesohippus was still walking on 3 toes, but its center toe was larger and bore most of the animal's weight. Pliohippus evolved during the Pliocene epoch about 5 million years ago, and was the first one-toed horse. It stood about 4 feet tall at the shoulders. Equus, our modern horse, evolved from Pliohippus. Horses again spread to Europe, Asia, South America, and Africa. About 10,000 years ago, horses died out in the Americas, but they were brought here again from Europe by the Spanish in the 16th century. The wild horses of the North American plains are descendants of the horses that were imported by the Spanish settlers.

How Did the Rhinoceros Evolve?
From a Small, Hornless Tapirlike Animal

As these tapirlike animals increased in size they developed large, bony knobs on their snouts. By the Oligocene they had evolved to giant-size, like Brontotherium. The largest land mammal that is known to exist was a hornless rhinoceros from Asia. It is called Indricotherium. It was over 16 feet high at the shoulder and weighed 8 times as much as a modern rhinoceros. It was the largest mammal of the Cenozoic Era. Another large mammal was the Balachiterium.

What Was the First Elephant Like?
It was Small and Did Not Have a Trunk

Moertherium, an early kind of elephant, was small, about the size of a pygmy hippopotamus, and lived in swampy areas. It did not have a trunk. Like other animals, the elephants increased in size as they evolved. Unlike giraffes and camels, which developed a long neck to help forage food and water, the elephant's neck became shorter and broader to support its heavy head. In order to eat and drink safely, later elephants evolved the long trunk.

> **FUN FACT: Prehistoric camels did not have humps because they did not live in the desert and did not need to store fat.**

If Mammals Developed on Land, When and Where Did Water Mammals Evolve?
About 46 Million Years Ago Near Africa

About 50 million years ago mammals returned to the seas. An early whale was called Basilosaurus and was over 60 feet long. Manatees and dugongs, also called sea cows, whose descendants are still living today, evolved about 45 million years ago. They ranged in size from 7 to 10 feet long. They had highly developed hind limbs, probably used as paddles, and they may have been seal-like in habit.

Where Did the First Whales Develop?
Near Africa

Scientists think that whales are descended from mesonychids, the doglike hunters that evolved during the Paleocene. As yet, there is no fossil record of all of the changes that had to have taken place for a land animal to evolve into a fish-eating water animal that was unable to live on land. There are two kinds of modern whales: toothed whales and baleen whales. Scientists think that they are both descendants of the early whales off the coast of Africa. After becoming fully adapted to water, whales were able to travel the seas all over the world.

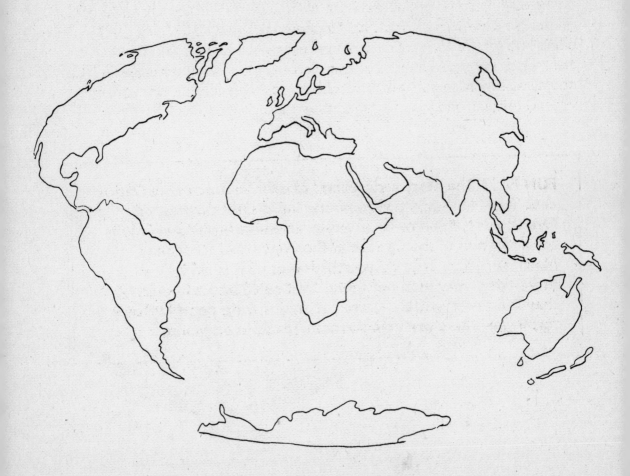

When Did the Earth's Climate Begin to Change?

About 38 to 25 Million Years Ago

During the Oligocene epoch, which followed the Eocene epoch, the climate on the earth became cooler and drier. Africa was isolated from the other continents. New forests and grasslands appeared where once only tropical plants had grown. Many early mammals unable to adapt to the new environment, died. Many new families of mammals emerged. Some mammals such as opossums, rats, mice, squirrels, and rabbits, were able to adapt to the changing environment, and their descendants are still living today.

FUN FACT: The most widespread of all mammals in the Oligocene were the early cud chewers, called Oreodonts. Most Oreodonts lived in or near water. Scientists have found more fossil remains of the Oreodont than any other mammal in North America. Why do you think that is? It could be that there were very many of them. Or it could be that because they lived near water, where conditions were good for fossil formation, there are now so many fossils to be found.

What Were the Most Important Plant Eaters of the Oligocene?

The Even-Toed Hoofed Mammals

The even-toed hoofed mammals are divided into two groups: pigs and cud chewers. One of the largest pigs was Dinohyus, which lived in North America and was almost the size of a hippopotamus.

Which Plant Eaters Evolved into Modern Camels, Giraffes, and Deer?

The Cud Chewers

Cud chewers that evolved in the Oligocene were the ancestors to camels, giraffes, and deer, but they looked very different from their modern counterparts. Most modern even-toed hoofed mammals have horns or antlers, but their Oligocene ancestors were hornless. Only Protoceras, a cud chewer that ranged from rabbit-sized to sheep-sized, had little bony growths on its head and snout. *Protoceras* means "first horn" or "first deer."

While the Plant Eaters Were Slowly Evolving Toward Modern Forms, What Were the Meat Eaters Doing?

Meat Eaters Were Dying Out

Modern meat eaters are divided into two groups: dogs and cats. The first cats were somewhat like modern civets and mongooses. The first dogs were similar to weasels. By the middle of the Oligocene, biting and stabbing cats had evolved. The biting cats were fast runners and killed their prey by pouncing on it and biting through its neck. The stabbing cats were larger and slower and used huge, daggerlike teeth to slash their prey.

The dog group also includes foxes, wolves, bears, pandas, badgers, raccoons, and weasels. All of these modern meat eaters were well established by the end of the Oligocene.

What Was the Miocene Period?
A Time When the Climate Became Even Cooler and Drier

During the Miocene period, from 25 to 5 million years ago, landmasses continued to move and give rise to many mountain ranges. North and South American mountains, which later were to become the Rockies and the Andes, were pushed up to new heights. India and Africa "crashed" into Eurasia, creating the great mountain ranges of the Himalayas and the Alps. The mammals of Africa were no longer separated from other mammals, and the plant-eating hoofed mammals moved into Africa. The Earth grew cooler, and grasslands expanded throughout. The water mass that was the Mediterranean Sea dried up. South America and Australia were still isolated.

DISCOVERY CORNER: When things evolve, they slowly change. Nonliving things can evolve, too! Check your library for pictures of cars, clothes, or houses from long, long ago. Can you see how these things have changed over the years? What will cars, clothes, or homes look like in the year 4000? In the year 8000? Draw pictures of the evolutions you imagine.

What Were the Chalicotheres?

They Were One of the Only Surviving Odd-Toed Hoofed Mammals in the Miocene.

Chalicotheres were heavy horse-sized animals related to titanotheres and horses. The chalicothere Moropus had a horselike head, a sloping back, and strong legs. Instead of hooves, Moropus had claws on its feet. Some scientists think that Moropus used these claws to dig up roots for food. Other surviving odd-toed hoofed mammals in the Miocene were horses, rhinoceroses, and tapirs.

What Was the Pliocene Epoch?
A Time When the World's Climate and Animals Became More Varied

During the Pliocene, 5 to 2 million years ago, South America was again joined to North America, and there was a massive exchange among mammals. During this time, mammals were more varied than they ever had been before—even more so than today! Even-toed hoofed mammals were very successful and evolved into their modern forms during the Miocene and Pliocene. The only odd-toed hoofed mammals surviving were horses, rhinoceroses, chalicotheres, and tapirs. There were many kinds of elephants. Rodents, dogs, and cats were also numerous. Toothless mammals called edentates, such as the armadillos, sloths, and giant anteaters, were found in North and South America. Primates continued to evolve in both South America and Africa. Some primates in Africa began to evolve more human-like characteristics. The world's climate continued to grow colder and colder as the Pleistocene, with its ice ages, approached.

What Was the Earth Like During the Pleistocene Epoch?

This Was the Time of the Ice Ages and the Age of Man

This period and time began about 2 million years ago and ended about 10,000 years ago. It was a time of great temperature changes from warm to cold and back to warm again. Great sheets of ice periodically covered almost ⅓ of the Earth's surface during the ice ages. Many animals lived in cold regions, but other moved to warmer climates. The warmer times between the ice ages were called "the interglacials." In order to survive the cold periods and the long trips, or migrations, many animals evolved to larger and stronger forms. Human beings continued to evolve during this period.

What Were the Large Mammals of the Pleistocene Like?

Most Were Very Large, and in the Cold Regions They Had Thick Coats of Fur

Many of the large plant eaters became well-adapted to the cold of the ice ages. The most famous were the woolly mammoth and the woolly rhinoceros. There were also giant versions of animals similar to those that exist today, such as the giant beaver, Irish elk, giant kangaroo, cave bear, giant ground sloth, and the Glyptodont, a giant armadillo-type mammal.

FUN FACT: Some Pleistocene mammals were rather small. While some animals were enormous during the Pleistocene epoch, a few were actually quite small. These animals lived on islands where food was scarce. Fossils of miniature versions of large mammals, such as dwarf mammoths and pygmy hippopotamuses, are often found on islands.

What Are the Rancho La Brea Tar Pits?

Fossil Deposits That Have Given Scientists an Incredible Number of Fossils from the Late Pleistocene Epoch

In Spanish, *brea* means "tar." Rancho La Brea contains shallow pools of black asphalt and water. The asphalt trapped animals and preserved their bones as fossils. Rancho La Brea is important because the fossil bones are so well preserved and because of the amazing variety of animals. The fossils from Rancho La Brea give scientists a very clear picture of life in Southern California during the late Pleistocene. In 1913 the Natural History Museum of Los Angeles County was given permission to excavate the fossils. The museum assembled and displayed many skeletons of the Pleistocene animals. Now all of the fossil material from Rancho La Brea is housed and exhibited at the George C. Page Museum of La Brea Discoveries.

Why Are There So Many Fossils in the Rancho La Brea Deposits?

Animals Were Lured into the Tar, Which Eventually Trapped Them

Whether they wandered into the tar to drink, feed, or flee from a predator, once stuck the animals probably cried out in distress, which lured others to the trap. Some may have come to help, while others, the meat eaters, came for an easy meal. Either way, most of them ended up as fossils, too.

What Are the Most Famous Animals from Rancho La Brea?

The Carnivores

There are more fossils of dire wolves from Rancho La Brea than of any other mammals. Dire wolves were slightly larger than wolves today, but they too probably hunted in packs or groups. This probably accounts for the large numbers found at Rancho La Brea. The most famous mammal from Rancho La Brea is the saber-toothed cat. The saber-toothed cat had huge canine teeth that looked like daggers with sawlike edges, which the animal used for stabbing or slashing its prey. Scientists think that when the saber-toothed cat attacked a large mammal (such as a mammoth, mastodon, or ground sloth), it would look for a vulnerable spot on the body of its prey, usually the neck or soft belly, then pounced. The cat would then hold on with its powerful front legs and stab or slash the animal, opening a large wound and allowing the prey to bleed to death. The saber-toothed cat is the official state fossil of California.

DISCOVERY CORNER: Look at your mouth in a mirror. Find the teeth on your upper jaw that are pointed and triangular-shaped. These are called your canines. Can you imagine what it would be like if your canines were 8 inches long like a saber-toothed cat's?

What Other Mammal Fossils Were Found in Rancho La Brea?

Many of the Major Groups of Pleistocene Mammals Are Represented by Fossils from Rancho La Brea

Ninety percent of the animal fossils from Rancho La Brea were meat eaters, mostly from the dog and cat families. The most famous fossils from Rancho La Brea are of dire wolves, saber-toothed cats, lions, bears, camels, deer, antelope, ancient bison, mastodons, mammoths, ground sloths, and many other smaller mammals such as shrews, rabbits, and rodents.

FUN FACT: Cave paintings show us that the woolly mammoth collected fat on its forehead in preparation for winter. The drawings depict a lumpy forehead ready for winter and a smaller head (and thinner body) in the spring.

Have Any Human Fossils Ever Been Found in Rancho La Brea?

Yes, Fossils of a Woman Have Been Found

These human fossils are known as La Brea Woman and are the only human fossils ever found at Rancho La Brea. The fossils are from an Indian woman who lived in California 3,000 years ago.

FUN FACT: Many scientists believe that the ancestors of the American Indians came from Asia to North America by crossing the same land bridge that many prehistoric mammals traveled.

What Were Humans Like in the Pleistocene?

Human Beings Not Only Continued to Adapt to their Environment But Developed Culture

The Miocene was primarily a time of a huge variety of very specialized animals. As the Earth's climate changed, mammals that could adapt to these changes survived. By the end of the Pliocene the pattern of evolution began to change. There was a trend toward animals that were more adaptable, and therefore better able to survive in a changing environment. Human beings are very adaptable mammals. They have not only learned to use fire and tools and to hunt, but have developed culture. By the middle of the Pleistocene, human beings were the masters of their environment.

DISCOVERY CORNER: Paleontologists study fossils to find out how animals lived a long time ago. Similarly, paleontologists and archaeologists study artifacts (items made by humans) to find out how past civilizations lived. Sometimes, people place a variety of items in a "time capsule" and store it so that others at a later date can find the capsule and learn about an earlier life. You can make your own time capsule. Start with a shoe box with a lid, then gather a variety of nonperishable items that tell about your life, such as a well-worn tennis shoe, ticket stubs to a movie, family snapshots, a report card, and a post-card from your vacation. Seal your time capsule and carefully mark it with the date. Put it away. Remember to open your time capsule in one, two, or five years!
